This Journal Belongs To:

Manufactured by Amazon.ca
Bolton, ON

41077938R00068